Mountains of Grace
By
Carolyn Davison

Copyright © Carolyn Davison 2019

The right of Carolyn Davison to be identified as the author of this work has been asserted by her in accordance with the Copyright, Designs and Patents Act, 1988

All rights reserved. This book is sold subject to the condition that it shall not, by way of trade or otherwise, be lent, re-sold, hired out or otherwise circulated in any form of binding or cover other than that in which it is published. No part of this book may be reproduced, whether by photocopy or by other means nor must any of the content be displayed on a website without prior permission from the author.

ISBN: 978-0-9561573-5-5

To the glory and honour Jesus Christ, who gave His life as a ransom for many.

To Adrian and Naomi Brake, such a blessing Thank you for your prayers and encouragement!

To Tim, a massive thank you for editing my poems

CAPTIVATE

Captivate my heart, O Lord;
Fill it with truth and grace.
That I may be like Jesus Christ,
When I see Him face to face.

Captivate my mind, O Lord,
And make me to be wise.
That I may know and do Your will,
Not ruled by worldly lies.

Captivate me with Your love,
That loving I may be.
Spirit fill my heart and mind,
For all eternity.

NOTHING BUT CHRIST IS WORTHY

The Lord must reign within my heart;
With Him, what can compare?
Possessing naught is blessedness
When the Lord God is reigning there!

The sins which I possess within
I sacrifice to God:
For naught is worthy of my praise,
But Jesus Christ, my Lord!

I raise my Ebenezer, Lord,
Within my sinful heart:
For naught will take away Your love,
And You will ne'er depart!

COME SEE

Come see the baby in His crib,
Wrapped in swaddling bands.
He is the One who rules the world -
Created by His hands.

All earth bow down!
All creation praise!
For the King of glory reigns!

Come see the Man who calms the storm;
He heals the deaf and blind;
He comes to save the lost and weak -
The lowliest of mankind.

All earth bow down!
All creation praise!
For the King of glory reigns!

Come see the Man upon the cross,
Pain written on His face.
He came to take our punishment -
He came to take our place.

All earth bow down!
All creation praise!
For the King of glory reigns!

Come see the tomb, an empty space;
The Saviour has conquered death!
He endured such suffering -
To give us spiritual breath.

All earth bow down!
All creation praise!
For the King of glory reigns!

Come see the King upon His throne;
He reigns in heaven above.
He calls a people for His own,
Who worship Him in love!

All earth bow down!
All creation praise!
For the King of glory reigns!

I AM

I AM the LORD of hosts,
Who reigns from heaven above.
My heart is full of peace and joy,
Blessings, grace and love.

I AM your Shield and Buckler;
A secret hiding place.
I come to you with kindness,
Gentleness and grace.

I AM a big strong Tower,
Safety from the storm;
Protection from the coldest hearts,
A place to keep you warm.

I AM a gentle Shepherd,
Who watches o'er My sheep.
I lift them up to My breast.
Them, safely I will keep.

I AM a powerful Banner;
My people I defend.
My Kingdom I am building,
Of it, there is no end.

I AM the Great Provider;
I give you all you need.
A smoking flax I will not quench
Nor break the bruisèd reed.

I AM the LORD, The Prince of Peace,
Making sinners kin -
Eternal life I give to them;
To heaven, they enter in.

I AM the Lord who sanctifies -
You're holy through My Son.
The victory over sin and death;
At Calvary it was won.

Come to Me all you who weep,
And I will give you rest.
You call Me Abba, Father;
Through Me you will be blessed.

I SHALL WANT FOR NOTHING

Nothing shall I ever want;
The Lord will guard my needs.
See Him on Golgotha's hill;
For me my Saviour bleeds.

He lies me down at His feet;
His Spirit nurtures me.
My dying Saviour all alone
Nailed to a cursèd tree.

I will not fear the evil
Which presses all around,
For my Redeemer died and suffered
On Calvary's sacred ground.

My head has been anointed
With the Holy Spirit's oil.
The blood from Jesus' stripes
Drops on creation's soil.

Goodness and mercy follow me,
Because of what You've done.
My hope is in eternity
In God's begotten Son.

I STOOD AT THE FOOT OF THE CRUEL CROSS

I stood at the foot of the cruel cross
And gazed at Your blood ridden face!
I stood there in awe and in wonder
At God's pure compassion and grace!
I knelt down and cried out for mercy;
My sins nailed You to that cruel tree!
You clothed me in God's holy glory,
When You died there at Calvary!

I stood and I looked up to heaven
And saw Your once piercèd side!
I stood there in awe and in wonder -
For me Great Jehovah had died!
You looked down and touched me with mercy -
Your love and Your grace set me free.
And one day I'll stand there in glory -
Because You died there, at Calvary.

I COME TO THE CROSS

I come to the cross, to be forgiven,
My sins on the Sinless One laid!
The debt I owed I could not fulfil,
But through Him my debt is paid.

To the cross, to the cross,
I come to the old rugged cross.
For my sins, to be cleansed
By the blood of the Lamb!
To the cross, to the cross
I come.

I come to the cross, to gain my dress;
Naked, He covers my shame.
My chains are loosed; I am set free;
Jesus, My Saviour, His Name.

To the cross, to the cross,
I come to the old rugged cross.
For my sins, to be cleansed
By the blood of the Lamb!
To the cross, to the cross
I come.

I come to the cross; my burdens lift;
My guilty soul bears guilt no more.
His blood avails; I am at peace.
He is Heaven's Eternal Door!

*To the cross, to the cross,
I come to the old rugged cross.
For my sins, to be cleansed
By the blood of the Lamb!
To the cross, to the cross
I come.*

I come to the cross, the place of wrath;
The punishment, meant for me,
Was laid upon my Saviour dear,
As He hung there at Calvary!

JESUS, ROCK OF OUR SALVATION

Jesus, Rock of our salvation,
Let us on You stand.
Jesus, cleft for our redemption,
Guide us with Your hand.

Jesus, Shepherd of Your people,
Help us hear Your voice.
Jesus, Bridegroom of the Church,
We praise You for Your choice.

Jesus, Bridge to our Heavenly Father,
Let us daily come.
Jesus, builder of our mansion;
Our eternal, heavenly home.

MAKE ME...

Make my life one of beauty, Lord;
Glorifying You!
Help me not to quench Your work,
In everything I do.

Make me more like Jesus, Lord;
Full of love and grace!
Help me to be holy, and see
My Saviour face to face.

Make me want to serve You, Lord,
Every single day!
Make me a useful servant
In all I do and say.

Make me want to sing your praise,
In good times, or in woe!
And if You call me to a task,
Help me to keenly go.

Make me an instrument of peace;
Please set my life apart -
To live one that is holy,
With a broken, contrite heart.

PRECIOUS SONS OF GOLD (BASED ON LAMENTATIONS 4:2)

More precious than expensive gem;
More precious than many other men.
More precious than a gift of old -
E'en more precious than the purest gold.

Oh Lord in heaven,
The mighty works of Your hands
Are seen in the Masterful work
Of Your creation.
We are the clay,
You are the Potter
Forming a people
From every nation.

So fragile the pots
Your mastery crafts,
But never would You
Break them.
Instead You hold them
In Your arms,
Never to forsake them.

Fashioned like a golden crown;
A Royal Diadem.
Clothed in garments
All divine -
A precious ruby gem.

Apple of Your caring eye,
Held in eternal arms.
Great Shepherd of Your
Wandering sheep -
They cannot come to harm.

A Shield and Fortress will You be,
As darkness surrounds Your Bride?
The gates of hell will not prevail;
Nor man's most arrogant pride.

BASED ON PSALM 23

I am a sheep and the Lord's my Shepherd;
Nothing shall I need.
To lush green pastures and cool streams
My belovèd Shepherd leads!

In paths of righteousness I take,
My soul He doth restore.
For His name's sake He does these things;
I cannot ask for more.

E'en though death may haunt my steps,
And the valley may be dark,
No evil shall I fear at all;
I'm in my Saviour's heart.

The Lord is with me all the days;
His promises are sure.
His rod and staff, they comfort me,
As long as life endures.

Enemies are all around,
But food You will provide.
Precious oil to anoint the head
Of Your chosen, perfect Bride!

How can I doubt Your promises?
In Your heart I am secure.
Goodness and mercy follow me,
And Your love always endures!

BASED ON PSALM 40

I sat in the darkness of the pit;
The blackness of my sin,
Swamped in my iniquity.
No way out and no way in.

I could not stand, for beneath my feet
Was a mass of slippery clay.
In my many trials and struggles,
I saw not the light of day.

I cried out to the heavens above,
To my Father and my Lord.
He listened to my pleading cries;
Kept the promises in His word.

He reached down into that pit,
And took me in His arms;
He set me on a sturdy rock -
I knew I'd not be harmed.

A song He gave me, in my mouth,
A new song in my heart.
I knew that He had saved me;
Now we'd never be apart!

That man who makes the Lord his trust
Blessings will abound;
Peace and joy and happiness
In him will be found.

BASED ON PSALM 1:1-4

Let us be blessed as men
Who love the law of God;
Who praise and glorify His name
And rest upon His word.

Let us be like the tree
Which drinks the waters deep,
And meditate upon God's word
And all His statutes keep.

Let us produce fruit
Which yields much heavenly good -
'Tis manna to the hungry soul;
Divine and filling food.

BASED ON EZEKIEL 34

Woe to you,
Shepherds of Israel:
My sheep you will not feed.
You leave them lost;
Their hunger burns -
Abandoned by your greed

Woe to you,
Keepers of sheep;
Your flock are prey to beasts.
They wander, lost
On hill and mount!
When will your treachery cease?

Woe to you,
Religious men,
Who lead your sheep astray!
Poisonous words
And evil deeds -
But there will come a day
When you will fear
The Mighty Lord
Whose strength you can't defeat,
Nowhere to run
Nowhere to hide
His judgement so complete.

Repent and turn
To David's Son,
The Great Shepherd of the sheep.
In pastures green
He lies you down,
And protects you in your sleep.

No longer lost,
No longer scared;
He loves with all His heart.
Safe in His arms,
He holds you close
And He will ne'er depart.

RIDE ON

"Ride on!" we hear the battle cry,
Triumphant to the end!
Our Captain of Salvation leads -
Our Saviour and our Friend!

We are more than conquerors
Over all our foes.
The banner of our Saviour
We follow where're He goes.

Through trials and temptations;
Through water or through flame,
His band of mighty soldiers
Praise His glorious name.

Ride on, ride on to victory -
The Celestial City is nigh.
Hosanna to the King of kings
Who reigns o'er the earth from high!

THE BRIDE

Who is this Bride so splendid?
She's been bought with a price.
Her beauty goes beyond the nations -
A dear and treasured wife.

Who is this Bride so belovèd?
Who looks upon her Groom,
As her Saviour and Redeemer;
Conqueror o'er sin's gloom.

Who is this Bride so precious?
More precious than a gem.
Adorned in robes of beauty;
Blessed more than other men.

Who is this Bride so cherished?
Her position is renown.
She wears not thorns upon her head,
But a glorious, jewelled crown.

This Bride is Jesus' people:
The ones He came here for.
He became a Sacrifice
To win her;
He became her open door.

Now all who come to God
Come through Jesus, His only Son,
To be adorned in wondrous splendour.
The victory He has won.

Victory over sin and death,
Damnation and the tomb.

THE VIRTUOUS WOMAN

Who is this wife
So rare and precious
Who has a worth above a gem?
Who is the man
Who safely trusts her?
He is above all other men.

Who is this wife
Who does him good;
Who works hard with her hands?
Who cooks with love -
She brings him food
From a myriad of lands.

Who is this wife
Rising at night
To feed those in her home?
She works with love
And tenderness -
With joy, and not a moan.

Who is this wife?
She sees a field;
She buys it for some vines,
To grow fresh grapes
So she can make
Some rare and precious wines.

Who is this wife
Who works all day?
Her lamp is lit all night!
She spins and weaves;
Makes fine clothes;
Her heart just shines with light.

Who is this wife
Who sees the need
Of those so poorly fed?
She reaches out
Her eager hands
To give them living bread.

Who is this wife
Who has no fear
Of snow within her breast?
Her family are
Always clothed
With the finest and the best.

Who is this wife
Of wisdom rare -
Kindness upon her tongue?
Glory, praise
And honour are hers
As a song of joy is sung!

Blessed is this wife
Who works
For the glory of her Lord!
Strength and virtue
She shall wear
And honour is her word!

Deceitful is all
Worldly charm;
Beauty passes away!
But the one who
Serves and obeys the Lord
A crown will wear one day.

THE GULF

There it is, so vast and empty,
Darkness covering such a span;
No way over for the person -
Massive gulf 'tween God and man.

Sin destroyed the pure communion
That God had with His Creation!
Gulf so dark, so vast, so empty,
Separating God from every nation.

There He stands in finest glory:
The One to come and bridge the span.
The One who willingly came from heaven;
The One true God who comes as Man.

Gulf so vast, so dark and empty,
Created at the awful Fall;
But there lies One to restore communion -
Tiny Babe in animal stall.

There it is so dark and empty;
No way to God; all seems a loss;
But on a hill outside the city
A man is nailed to the cross!

The gulf so dark, lonely, empty
Is being breached by this Man -
Dying to provide us with redemption,
Making a way across the span!

There He hangs dead on the tree -
God who came from human womb -
But the gulf is being covered
As He lies in darkest tomb.

Oh the cross, so evil, wicked
God had used to complete His plan!
The Sinless One - He now is risen -
Through His death we cross the span!

THE NEW COVENANT

Not to the burning altar come,
With sacrifice of blood;
But to the cross of Calvary
Our Saviour came in love.

Not to the laver, made of bronze,
To wash ourselves from sin;
But at the cross this was fulfilled.
Come now, and enter in.

Not to the lamp to ignite the flame,
Nor burn the incense there,
For now we have God's holy Light;
The incense is our prayer.

Not to the table with twelve loaves,
Nor to the Mercy Seat,
For Jesus is the Bread of Life;
God's mercy is complete!

Not with the robes of glorious hue,
Nor Pomegranates at our feet,
For Jesus Christ, our Sacrifice,
Is now our Great High Priest.

No Tabernacle, nor temple now;
Just Jesus Christ alone.
The Holy of Holies: God's Spirit
Makes us His blessèd home.

THE SAVIOUR - MY HOPE

When darkness seems as black as night,
And worries pierce my soul -
The Saviour prays and intercedes;
He comes to make me whole.

When trials abound in every sphere,
And burdens weigh me down -
The Saviour takes me in His hand;
His glory is my crown.

When worldly things pull and press,
And Satan steals my joy -
The Saviour holds me in His arms;
His strength is my alloy.

When sin abounds and fear endures,
Temptations lay me low -
The Saviour comes with gentle words.
"Don't fret, I love you so!"

THERE IS FORGIVENESS

Christian:

>I've been a terrible Christian;
>I've sinned against the Lord!
>I want to give up everything;
>Including reading the word.

Satan:

>"You've been an awful person;
>You've been stupid and unwise;
>You're too bad to come to Jesus!"
>Whispers Satan with his lies.

Christian:

>Where will I find forgiveness
>For everything I've done?
>I know that God sent Jesus,
>His only begotten Son.

Satan:

>But surely you've been too wicked!
>Even though you're born again,
>Does God truly want to forgive
>Vile and sinful men?

God answering the Christian:

You may have been a terrible Christian;
Yes, you've sinned against the Lord.
Remember who you are in Christ -
Come, turn and read the word!

God answering Satan:

My people may do awful things,
But I'm the Potter and they're the clay.
I am always working in their lives,
To purify them all one day.

God answering the Christian:

You will always find forgiveness
At the foot of the wooden cross,
Where Jesus took on all your sins
And cancelled out My wrath.

God answering Satan:

There are none too wicked
Who can't find forgiveness there;
At the foot of the cruel cross
All their sins Christ did bear.

God to Christians:

> So come, discouraged Christian,
> Repent, and turn to Me!
> Remember who you are in Christ:
> You are His eternally!

UPON THE CROSS

Upon the cross our Scapegoat hung:
All our sins on Him were laid -
Into the wilderness of death,
All our debts now paid!

Upon the cross, atonement made!
God's wrath burned upon He.
The Lamb was slain for our sakes,
As He died on Calvary.

Upon the cross, the Law fulfilled
By the One of purity!
Our sins destroyed,
Now peace with God:
Our souls have been set free!

Upon the throne He intercedes -
Our glorious, heavenly King!
Risen, triumphant, glorified!
His praise we all must sing!

IMAGINE

Imagine there's no Yahweh.
Imagine if you can;
There'd be no earth or planets;
No animals or man

Come on, imagine, people, there'd be nothing here

Imagine there's no Jesus
If that's what ya wanna do;
Then what are our years for;
Christmas, Easter too?

Come on, imagine people, you would not celebrate

You
You may say I'm a dreamer,
But I'm not the only one
'Cos millions of people
Believe in God's own Son!

Imagine there's no religion;
Life still wouldn't be fair.
War would still rage around us;
People wouldn't care!

Come on, imagine people, you have to have belief

You

You may say I'm a dreamer,
But I'm not the only one
'Cos millions of people
Believe in God's own Son!

BE NOT ASHAMED

Be not ashamed of the Gospel;
It's the power of God's Word.
It brings light and salvation
Wherever it is heard.
It illuminates the darkness;
Gives life unto the dead;
Hope to all the hopeless;
Frees those who live in dread.

Be not ashamed of Calvary;
The cross is where we stand,
When sin and trials oppress us
And life's like sinking sand.
We gain a robe of righteousness;
A crown upon our head;
A garment of salvation;
And a feast of Living Bread.

Be not ashamed of Jesus;
His blood was shed for me.
The Prisoner hung upon the cross,
That I might be set free.
The hands which hold me underneath
Bear wounds of lasting love,
That I may spend eternity
With Him in heav'n above.

BE STRONG AND OF GOOD COURAGE

Be strong and of good courage;
The battle is the Lord's!
Put on your holy armour
And wield your two edged sword.
Stand firm with feet unslipping,
Your belt of truth secure.
Keep marching unto Zion;
You're in a holy war!

Be strong and of good courage;
The battle has been won!
Jehovah saw the triumph
Of His belovèd Son.
His heel was bruised at Calv'ry,
Thorns rested on His brow,
But Jesus, King of glory,
Is interceding now.

Be strong and of good courage
The battle soon will cease!
Our Captain of Salvation
Will bring His people peace.
Let not your heart be troubled;
Believe on Him alone.
He is the Lord of glory,
The Master Cornerstone.

Be strong and of good courage;
The Lord reigns from on high.
He is the mighty victor;
He knows our inward sighs.
His promises are steadfast;
His love is firm and sure.
His shadow is our refuge;
We're His forevermore.

Be strong and of good courage;
Though trouble may abound,
Our peace, eternal refuge,
In Jesus may be found.
He is our Holy Shelter;
He is our Blessèd Calm.
He is our strength in weakness,
Our Shadow from all harm.

COME TO THE LORD

Come to the LORD, you fearful;
Cast all your cares on Him!
The LORD will give you comfort!
His praises we shall sing!
He leads us like a Shepherd,
For we have gone astray.
He takes us to green pastures;
We sing His praise each day.

O grave, your boast is silent;
O death, your sting is gone.
For Jesus Christ is reigning!
We'll sing a victory song!
Come worship Him with gladness;
Rejoice with Psalms of praise!
For over us He's singing!
He keeps us all our days.

HELP ME TO BE MORE CHRIST-LIKE

Help me to be like Jesus Christ,
In everything I do.

Help me to be more holy.
And truly worship You.

Help me to work for Jesus,
Not for other men.

Help me to shine for You, Lord.
Time and time again.

Help me produce good fruit
Upon the Holy Vine.

Help me to love you more each day.
For Saviour, You are mine.

IN DEATH – IN CHRIST

In death there is no first;
In death there is no second;
In death there is no third;
Death doesn't distinguish between classes.

In death there is no black;
In death there is no white;
In death there is no olive;
Death doesn't distinguish between skin colour.

In death there is no man;
In death there is no woman;
In death there is no children;
Death doesn't distinguish between male or female,
Young or old.

Death, the great enemy, isn't fussy
About who it takes.
When your time has come,
You will have no choice!

Rich or poor,
Fat or thin,
Black or white,
Woman or man,
We are all born
To live, then die!

In Christ there is no first;
In Christ there is no second;
In Christ there is no third;
Christ doesn't distinguish between the classes.

In Christ there is no black;
In Christ there is no white;
In Christ there is no olive;
Christ doesn't distinguish between skin colour.

In Christ there is no man;
In Christ there is no woman;
In Christ there is no children;
Christ doesn't distinguish between male or female,
Young or old.

Christ, the Creator, Sustainer of all
Came to save those who call
On His name for forgiveness true!
Could He be calling YOU?

Rich or poor,
Fat or thin,
Black or white,
Woman or man,
We can live for Christ -
Eternally with Him!

FOR WHAT DOES IT PROFIT...

For what does it profit a man,
If he dedicates his life to things -
Sets his heart on raising cash,
But knows not the King of kings?

For what does it profit a man,
If he stores up treasures on earth –
Buying houses, cars and such,
But knows not of new birth?

For what does it profit a man,
If he gains the praise of all –
But closes up his inner ear
When the Saviour calls?

Jesus says:
"I am the way, the truth, the life";
Through no other you can come.
But joy, and peace and rest He gives –
In an eternal heavenly home!

No possessions or people
Can fill that aching empty void!
When Jesus fills the desolate heart -
Full life can be enjoyed!

THE CHIEF PRIEST

The chief priest entered once a year,
Into that holy place;
An atonement for the people made:
The promise of God's grace.

A spotless bull, without a mark,
Its life - a sacrifice;
Its blood upon the Mercy Seat:
A shadow of Jesus Christ.

The incense burned upon the altar
Rose to Heaven's courts.
The prayers of every contrite saint
Never come to nought.

Money paid - a ransom due;
Everyone to give.
Ransom paid at Calvary;
The chosen are to live.

THE GIFT

This is not a gift
With golden bow,
Sitting beneath
The old pine tree,
Wrapped with paper,
Sealed with tape
And only just for me.

This is not a gift
Made with hands
Which moth
and rust destroy.
A jewellery piece;
Clothes of wool;
A child's most favoured toy.

This is not a gift
To be forgot':
Hidden away
For none to see.
Unwanted game;
Disliked perfume,
From under the Christmas tree.

He is God's Gift:
Incarnate,
In a manger laid.
Wrapped in swaddling
Bands of cloth;
To the world -
He gave

He is God's gift
Not made with hands!
No man can e'er destroy.
The King of glory
Came to save
Man, woman,
Girl and boy

He is the greatest gift from God!
A Redeemer
from on high.
King of angels;
Devils; men –
To Jesus
Sinners fly.

One day the Greatest Gift for man
Will return with trumpet blast.
Surrounded by His heavenly host
The King will return
At Last!

THE TRUE WONDER OF CHRISTMAS

PART 1:

What is the true wonder of Christmas?
Is it the tinsel on the tree?
The branches made of needles?
The baubles hanging free?

What is the true wonder of Christmas?
Is it the wreaths upon the doors?
The garlands on the mantle?
A man called Santa Claus?

What is the true wonder of Christmas?
Is it the thought of gifts for me?
The rush to buy all presents?
The adverts on TV?

What is the true wonder of Christmas?
Is it the lights in every street?
The children in their school plays?
The chocolates, nuts and sweets?

PART 2:
In Bethlehem, a babe was born;
Through Him, the world has light.
He comes to end the darkness;
To do away with night.

In Bethlehem in Judah,
Three gifts were given there;
Gold for a king and myrrh for death
And frankincense so rare.

In Bethlehem, Ephrathah
No wreaths upon the door;
But a baby in a manger:
For us He became poor.

On Calvary, Golgotha,
No tinsel on that tree,
But a crown of thorns –
Upon the head
Of the One who set me free.

COME MEET

Come meet the tiny baby
Lying in His crib.
The one who created man
And woman from his rib.

Come meet the young boy now
Talking to men so wise.
The answers that He gave them
Caused such great surprise.

Come meet the mighty Healer
Who reigns over disease;
His power conquers demons -
Who fall upon their knees.

Come meet the powerful conqueror!
On the cross He took your sin.
No longer condemned to death –
We can enter in!

Come meet the Heavenly Father,
The One who gave you life.
Through Jesus Christ you come to Him!
Peace we have, not strife.

EMPTY - FULL

Come to the crib in Bethlehem town;
Where is the babe,
Lying still?
Empty of Jesus;
He's a grown man now,
Climbing Calvary's hill!

Come to the cross on Golgotha mount;
Where is the Man,
Dying soon?
Empty of Jesus;
He's wrapped in grave clothes,
Lying in a dark, cold tomb!

Come to the grave hewn out of rock;
Where is the Saviour,
Lying down?
Empty of Jesus;
He sits in the throne room,
Wearing a kingly crown!

Come to the Saviour,
No longer a babe,
No longer a man on the cross;
Conquering death,
Defeating our sin;
Come to gain fullness,
Not loss.

HE TOOK ON FLESH

Your Creator hands so tiny
Gripped Your mother's fingers.
The mouth which breathed
The world into being
Formed its first word.
The One who wrestled Jacob
At Peniel
Stumbled with His first steps.

Oh Mighty God,
You entered into our world -
That we might enter
Into Your Kingdom!

Oh Mighty Saviour,
You took on flesh,
That we might one day
Be with You in eternity!

Oh Mighty Conqueror,
You took on death
At Calvary
That we wouldn't have to die!

Oh Mighty King,
You rose triumphant
That Your glory
May also be ours!

Those Creator hands so tiny
Became hands which bore the nails.
The mouth which breathed
The world into being
Breathed its final triumphant words
"It is finished!"
The One who wrestled with Jacob
Crushed the serpent's head.
Death has no sting,
The grave no victory;
Death and grave: now dead!

A PLACE PREPARED

A Place Prepared for Heaven's Great King:
No palace, no castle, no songs to sing -
Just a stable and a manger bare;
A lowly place, to lie Him there.

A Place Prepared for Heaven's High Priest:
No house, no bed, no sumptuous feast -
Just a cross on a lonely hill!
Saviour Divine - men did kill.

A Place Prepared for Heaven's slain Lamb:
No pomp, no honour, for the Great I Am -
Just an empty tomb sealed with a stone!
Our Lord eternal lay there alone.

A Place Prepared for Heaven's belovèd Son:
No sin, no iniquity, no unrighteous one!
A golden throne, a diadem:
Blessèd Mediator for chosen men.

A Place Prepared for all who see:
No condemnation - only purity.
Each chosen child: no war, no strife;
Only peace and love. Eternal life.

So come, prepare your heart today;
Jesu's death cast your sins away.
The gift is FREE: no cost nor loss;
The price was paid at Calvary's cross.

Turn to Jesus, forsake your sin;
The gate is there: come, enter in!
The Prince of Peace has made a way -
Come to Him! Do not delay!

O LITTLE STAR

O little star of Bethlehem
Looking down on the world of men.
O little star, what do you see?
A tiny baby's nativity.

O little star high in the sky
Watching all the world go by.
O little star, what can you hear?
Angels praising the baby, dear.

O little star shining bright
Giving the world beautiful light.
O little star, what do you say?
Christ the Saviour was born today.

THE SHEPHERDS ON THE HILL

The shepherds on the hill
Were guarding all their sheep.
The people in the town below
Were in their beds, asleep.

The shepherds on the hill
Felt sleepy in the night.
But soon the sky lit up
With an angel, oh so bright.

The shepherds on the hill
Were scared as scared can be,
But the angel said "Fear not;
Come and listen to me!"

The shepherds on the hill
Heard what the angel said.
"A King is born in Bethlehem
With a manger for His bed!"

The shepherds on the hill
Saw more angels sing.
They worshipped baby Jesus,
Our Saviour and our King.

The shepherds on the hill
Went to Beth'lem town
To see this tiny King
Who didn't wear a crown.

They left their sheep behind;
Went down to find the child,
Who came to save us from our sin,
Who was so meek and mild.

The shepherds saw the baby,
Lying in His crib.
They knew He was the only one
Who could all their sins forgive.

They went away rejoicing;
Their hearts were filled with joy,
As they tenderly remembered
That tiny baby boy.

CHRISTMAS TIME

Christmas is a time for giving.
A time for joy.
A time for living.

Christmas is a time for meeting.
A time for friendships.
A time for greeting.

Christmas is a time for emotion.
A time for remembrance.
A time for devotion.

Christmas is a time in history.
A time written down
For eternity.

Christmas is a time to see a boy.
A time of birth.
A time of joy.

Christmas is a time of our Father's giving.
A time of love.
A time of living.

Christmas is a time for praising,
Of angels' songs -
Hallelujahs raising!

Christmas is a time for thought
Of the Gift God gives
Which can't be bought.

Christmas is a time to receive
The gift of life
Only God can give.

Christmas is a time which leads
To a certain place
Called Calvary.

If it wasn't for that time in history,
There would be no gifts;
No lit up tree;
No children singing
Christmas songs;
No Man who came
To right our wrongs.

Let us remember this Christmas time,
That Jesus came
To make Him mine;
He lived a life
We could never live,
To offer a gift
No one else could give.

FINDING WHAT YOU WILL – AND WON'T

You won't find a queen
Giving birth to a prince,
In a palace of silver and gold;
You will find a young maiden
Giving birth to a son,
In a stable so draughty and cold.

You won't find a cradle
Lined with rich padded silk,
Nor a pillow of scarlet or red;
You will find a manger;
A baby lies there,
Only straw for His delicate head.

You won't find the richest
Or the powerful of men
Visiting that baby so fair;
You will find some poor shepherds
With their gift of a lamb,
In that stable so mean and so bare.

You won't find a priest
Or a pharisee or scribe
Going to a place so cold;
You will find pagan kings
With gifts they did bring:
Frankincense, myrrh and gold.

You won't find a leader
Wearing a crown
Sitting on an earthly throne;
You will find the Saviour,
The Creator of the World,
Dying to call a people His own.

You won't find a light
In the dark heart of men,
Until the truth breaks them free;
You will find a man
With wounds in His hands -
He got them at Calvary!

THE BRIGHT MORNING STAR

I looked and saw the baby small
Lying in a stable bare.
His head was resting on the straw
No royal robes to wear.
The stench rose up and touched his nose;
It was likened to our sin!
The baby came to die for us;
He is the King of kings!

The shepherds sat in fields at night
With darkness all around!
The silence broke; with heavenly song:
The angels' joyful sound.
The darkness of the world will break,
For the Light of Salvation's come!
The Saviour of the world is here
To take His children home!

The wise men came from lands afar
Bearing presents for the King!
They brought gold and frankincense and myrrh:
The future they did bring!
The Heavenly Babe, the Morning Star,
To a darkened world brings light!
Accept the Saviour as your own;
He dispels the inward night!

GENTLE BABY – DYING LAMB – RISEN SAVIOUR

Gently formed in maiden's womb
The Redeemer of mankind.
Small and weak and helpless
Being formed to heal the blind.

Tiny arms and tiny legs
Stretching in the womb -
Being formed to die for us;
To defeat death in the tomb.

Gentle babe, no kingly robes;
Swaddling band as humble sheet.
Naked in birth; naked in death
Nails will pierce His feet.

Fingers grasping Mary's hand;
Smile upon His face.
Nails driven through His palms -
He dies to take our place!

Safely in His mother's arms;
No love for Him she lacks.
Becoming sin for all He calls -
His Father turns His back.

Beautiful babe in animal stall;
Life in every breath.
Lying in a darkened tomb
Conquering hell and death.

Heavenly babe lying still;
Prophetic gifts are given.
Tomb lies empty;
The Saviour lives!
He intercedes in heaven.

THE PRECIOUS GIFT

No shining tinsel in the stall,
No Christmas wreaths upon the wall,
No lights nor tree, no singing stranger;
Just a small babe in a manger.

No decorations in the stable,
No plump turkey on the table,
No moist pudding or Christmas cake;
But a babe who came for our sake.

No ringing bells in church steeple,
No celebration, nor laughing people,
No stockings, no baubles on the tree;
Just a babe who was from eternity.

No pomp offered to the King,
No rich palace for Him to live in;
Just a manger and a stall,
For the only Precious Gift of all.

No religious leader came to Him;
But shepherds and some wise kings.
A lowly place of manger and stall,
For the only Precious Gift of all.

THERE IS A TIME

Christmas is a time for giving;
A time for self-sacrifice;
A time of fun and laughter;
A joyous time for living.

Christmas is a time for sharing;
A time for songs;
A time for eating and drinking;
A time to start caring.

Christmas is a time for family and friends;
A time for peace;
A time for lights;
A time we wished there was no end.

Christmas is a time we should remember;
A time to reflect;
A time to recall!
It's not just another day in December.

In the fulness of time God sent
His only begotten Son,
Who lived a life we could not,
To Calvary He went.

In the fulness of time He will come again
From the place beyond our comprehension
He will take His redeemed
To the place where there is no time.

THE NIGHT BEFORE CHRISTMAS (1)

'Twas the night before Christmas
And I think we can bet
That millions of people
Have gone into debt;
To buy special presents,
Some big and some small.
Some will be accepted;
Some not at all!

Cupboards are loaded
With excesses of food;
Fridges with beer,
Other alcohol too.
Children, excited,
Won't go to bed late;
They try to be good –
Make everyone a mate.

Nothing will change
As they all grow,
'Cos Christmas is about
Goodwill, as you know.
So if someone knocks over
Your drink in the bar
You brush it aside,
Just for one day a year.

Have you ever stopped and wondered
Why it's not the same
As other celebrations
You could care to name?
Is it really about
A fat man in red coat;
Lights, decorations
And carnival floats?

Is it about getting yourself
Into debt?
Getting uptight
And starting to fret?
Have I bought this
And have I bought that?
I mustn't forget
My dear pet cat!

There's far more to Christmas
Than you could ever expect.
A Man came to pay for
Your life full of debt;
He came to this earth
To live a life we could not;
He paid for our sins
When He went to the cross!

He was born in a stable,
A manger for a crib.
He taught many people
How to love and forgive.
He even loves those
Who mock Him and tease,
And try to destroy Him
By the lives that they lead.

For 2,000 years people have
Tried to destroy
Every man, every woman,
Every girl, every boy,
Who truly believes
That He is the One
Who is their Redeemer
And God's only Son!

But for 2,000 years
The church still goes on;
No liberal, no commie
Can destroy God's own Son.
So whether you believe
He came to save YOU!
Have a very Merry Christmas
And Happy New Year too!

THE NIGHT BEFORE CHRISTMAS (2)

'Twas the night before Christmas
And all through the nation
Christians were gathered
With joy and elation,
To celebrate the coming
Of their glorious King,
Who came to clean up
Their hearts full of sin.

He humbled Himself;
Came as a babe in a crib
Living on earth
To love and forgive;
Healing the sick,
The lame and the blind,
The demon-possessed,
And the feeble of mind.

He taught many people
Redemption and grace,
To love one another
Through the trials they face.
He went to the cross
To show His pure love;
To take on the wrath
Of His Father above!

After three days in the tomb
He arose!
Victor o'er death
And the vile hellish foes -
Now He's ascended
To heaven above -
The Great Intercessor
With a heart full of love!

So come, let's remember
On this Christmas Day,
The wonderful Saviour
Who in a crib lay -
Will one day return
No longer a babe,
To gather His people
He joyfully saved.

THE PRINCE OF PEACE

The Prince of Peace from glory came,
To a world full of strife.
He came to save and justify,
So that sinners may have life.

The Prince of Peace to a stable came,
A manger for His bed.
A jealous king and religious men
Wanted Jesus dead!

The Prince of Peace to a region came,
Where soldiers marched the streets.
Oppressed by sin and iniquity?
Jesus touches all He meets.

The Prince of Peace, to a hill He came
With a cross of shame and grief,
To take our sins upon Himself
And destroy our unbelief.

The Prince of Peace in a tomb was laid;
The crushed dragon thought he'd won.
But only Jesus' heel was bruised -
He rose the Glorious Son!

The Prince of Peace; in Heaven He sits:
The Lamb for sinners slain.
Eternal Son; Judah's Lion -
Forever He will reign.

THERE'S NO ROOM – THERE'S ALWAYS ROOM

THE WORLD:
There's no room at the inn for You;
No peace to sleep and rest!
Go and lie in a creature's trough;
We're sure that will be best!

There's no room in my heart for You;
It's full of sin and hate!
I'll do what I think is best for me –
God and heaven can wait!

There's no room in the world for You;
We're happy with war and strife!
We'll curse and swear; do what we want –
Even take Your life!

GOD'S GRACE:
There's always room at the cross for you!
Dear sinner, the Lord says, "Come!
For I will make you heirs with Christ,
And heaven will be your home!"

There's always room in God's heart for you;
He sent His Son in love!
He died because you are His joy;
You have a home above!

There's always room in heaven for you;
A place of peace and rest;
A table laid with the finest food;
A home where you'll be blessed!

LOOKING AT THE CROSS

When I look at the Cross
I see my Saviour there:
A crown of thorns upon His head;
Blood matted in His hair.

Nails in His feet and hands;
Sweat upon His brow;
Satan crushed beneath His feet!
Where is his victory now?

A beam stands upright to the heavens,
A cross bar parallel to earth;
Without the death of Jesus Christ
There would be no rebirth.

The veil is ripped from God to man;
Creation groans and quakes,
As Jesus dies upon this cross.
Atonement for us He makes.

Darkness spreads across the world
As God forsakes His Son!
Why have You forsaken Me?
But redemption's work is done.

"It is finished!" is His cry,
As He bows His head and dies.
He took my sins upon Himself,
When He was crucified!

Three days He lay in the cold, dark grave -
Defeating death and sin.
The Bridge to God is opened up;
Now many can enter in!

Now that tomb of Christ is empty;
He has risen from the dead.
He intercedes in heaven,
For the Church, of which He's head!

ARISE

Awake, O Church, Awake,
Soldiers of the Lord.
Arise, gird up your loins;
Wield your 2-edged sword.

Arise, O Church, Arise;
Put on your breastplate bright.
Protect your heart from the Evil One
Who is dark as darkest night.

Stand, O Church, Stand;
Prepare your gospel feet
To take the word to all around -
Everyone that you meet.

Guard, O Church, Guard
The truth and bind it round;
Store it in your heart,
Where the Holy Spirit's found!

Renew, O Church, Renew
The wisdom of your mind.
Put on your golden helmet:
Love and truth combined!

Defend, O Church, Defend;
Take up your shield of faith.
With it quench the fiery darts
Of the one who has no grace.

I WILL REST IN YOU ALONE

The Lord's my Rock and Hiding Place;
He is my refuge from all harm.
He shelters me beneath His mighty wings;
He holds me within His arms.

I will rest in you alone
I will rest in you alone;
You are my Rock; My Fortress; Hiding Place,
And you will guide me home.

"Fear not! For you are Mine;
You are washed as white as snow.
I will never leave nor forsake you;
I'm with you where'er you go!"

I will rest in you alone…

WOULD YOU GO THROUGH THIS FOR ME?

Would You go through this for me?
For me, O Lord and King?
Would One so pure and holy
Really suffer for MY sin?

Would You endure the loss of friends;
The loneliness and isolation?
Would You, O Lord, be mocked,
And be totally forsaken?

Would You endure the scourging whips;
The nakedness and shame,
So that Your Church could be Your Bride
And bear Your Holy Name?

Would You endure the searing pain,
The hunger and the thirst,
So that Your people would not die
But rejoice in joy and mirth?

Would You endure the Father's wrath,
Taking on our sinful chains,
So that You would have an holy people
Who with You would reign?

I can scarcely understand it;
I can scarcely believe it's true.
The One so pure and Holy -
My sins You would undo?

Jesus came to take the wrath;
The loneliness and shame;
Be forsaken and beaten,
So we may have His name.

Jesus came to be denied;
He stood condemned instead.
He came to lose His closest friends,
Who were fearful, lacked faith and fled!

He came to thirst, and hunger feel;
To bear the Father's rage;
The sinless One took on our sin,
Redeeming from age to age!

He:
still forgives;
changes lives;
We look to Him
for everything!
Redemption is completely free!
We do not have to work or toil!
As we are, we come to the cross.
He can set us:
free from the
darkness life
brings, from
sadness and
sorrow & pain.
He brings us
Into newness
of life and love
and heals our
broken hearts

THE JOURNEY

From the glorious splendour of heaven
You came to your mother's womb,
To live a servant's life on earth;
Your journey - an empty tomb.

From the adoration of angels rejoicing,
To a world full of sin, pain and loss;
A time of mock trial and scorning!
Your journey - a cruel wooden cross.

From the fellowship of Your dear Father,
To a people in need of much pardon.
Such anguish, no joy, and deep sorrow;
Your journey - a dark, lonely garden.

But rejoice in the journey of Jesus;
Without it our God would be hidden;
No salvation; no peace with the Father!
Rejoice! Jesus Christ is now risen!

Cry out "Hosanna in the highest!"
For Jesus now sits on the throne.
His journey of pain and of sorrow
Was travelled that He would atone!

Be filled with great adoration,
For King Jesus rules all the globe!
He's trodden the paths of great suffering;
He's travelled the cold lonely road.

His life brings good news of salvation;
His death brings us peace with our God.
Give thanks to the Son of His Father
For life's weary road He has trod!

MASTER

Master over all creation;
Master over storm and sea;
Master over deaf and mute;
But is He Master over me?

Master over crippled men;
Master, making blind to see;
Master over Satan's demons,
But is He Master over me?

Master over vile sinners;
Master, while on Calvary's tree;
Master; Lo, the grave can't hold Him,
But is He Master over me?

THE POWER OF A WORD

We got in the boat;
The sea was calm,
But soon a tempest arose.
Our Lord and Master was sleeping;
The waves splashing over our toes!

The wind howled around;
The waves rose like walls,
But Jesus was tired and slept.
What shall we do? We're all going to die!
We wailed; we mourned; we wept.

We went to the Lord
And shook Him awake.
"We're perishing; we need to be saved!"
"Why do you fear, you of little faith?"
With a word, He calmed wind and wave.

We sat in the boat;
The sea was calm.
The tempest obeyed its Master.
In wind, wave or trial;
Temptation; denial,
The Lord rules o'er every disaster.

BROKEN – WHOLE

[GOOD FRIDAY]

Broken men,
With a broken plan
Plot to destroy
The Son of Man.

Broken disciple,
With a broken heart
Takes some silver;
Tears himself apart.

Broken watch,
With a broken sleep.
Jesus prays,
And with blood He weeps.

Broken Saviour;
Broken friends have fled.
All alone,
Facing the ultimate dread.

Broken court,
With the broken trial.
Made up case;
Lots of lies, so vile!

Broken soldiers,
With a broken game;
Gambling for clothes;
Blaspheming His Name!

Broken thief,
With a broken life.
His conscience pricked
With the Spirit's knife.

Broken serpent;
Broken on that tree!
Death swallowed up
In Jesus' victory!

Broken veil,
In that soon broken place!
Now ALL who come through Jesus
Will see God, face to face!

Broken creation,
Broken as He died.
"My God, why am I forsaken?"
The Saviour's final cry!

Broken Redeemer;
Body broken for me,
As He takes God's wrath
At Calvary!

Broken women,
And broken men
Thought they would never
See Him again

Broken Light;
Broken Son;
Broken day;
The final work was done!

[RESURRECTION SUNDAY]

Broken morning
At a broken tomb!
The grave, for the Saviour,
Didn't have any room!

"He is risen! He is risen!"
The angel cries!
No more death; no more broken!
Come! Wipe your eyes!

Salvation is here;
Jesus no more bleeds!
In the heavens, for His people,
He now intercedes.

For the sinful, for the wicked
Jesus bled and died!
No sin too great and vast
For Jesus' sacrifice!

Come, come and gather
At the foot of the cross.
There is so much to gain
That will outweigh the loss:

Heaven's gates are open,
To welcome in the Bride,
Because of the one condemned -
The Lord, crucified.

The Redeemer sits in glory,
Sceptre in His hand;
Death and sin are broken!
Redemption through the lands!

The crown of thorns is broken!
Crown of glory on His head!
Life for those who believe on him!
Hope, and no more dread!

THE ONE

The One who wore the crown of thorns
Upon his blood stained brow
Wore those thorns so that we
Could wear a crown of glory now.

The One who had nail pierced hands
And had agony in His soul
Bore those wounds so that we,
In Spirit, could be made whole.

The One who bore the darkest sky,
Dark as the blackest night,
Took our sins upon Himself,
So we could live in light.

The One who hung all alone
On that vile, accursed cross
Hung in love and tenderness,
So we wouldn't suffer loss.

The One who bowed His weary head
And gave up His soul that day
Lifts up the heads of everyone
Who will follow in His way.

The One who lay dead in the tomb
Rose up in victory,
So that those who come and follow Him
Live for eternity!

THE PATH WE TREAD

The path we tread is narrow;
Is narrow along the way.
We journey onward to heaven,
Where the King of glory waits.

In His hands He bears the wounds
Of His love shown at Calvary.
The feet which were pierced for my sins
Bear the nail marks meant for me.

The path we tread leads to glory,
A place prepared by Him:
No more tears; only joy; no more sorrow -
Our hearts set free from sin.

On His head no more thorns of mocking;
No more blood on His furrowed brow,
But a robe so bright and spotless
And a crown of glory now!

CAUGHT

Your life felt so empty!
You needed a man
To fill up your heart,
Like no other one can.

You felt very lonely!
You wanted into his life!
Even though he was married
To a beautiful wife!

So you dressed in rich garments;
Put make-up on your face.
You wanted to steal him;
Take up his wife's place.

Adorning your hair
With oil and with jewels;
You thought you were safe
And that you were nobody's fool!

So in the light of the day,
You met up with this man!
You thought you were loved
By the touch of his hand!

Caught in the act,
There was nowhere to run!
The shame of being caught,
In the heat of the sun!

You knew what the score was,
When you set out to tempt!
The law says you must be stoned;
You are not exempt!

The Pharisees grabbed her
And brought her to the Son.
"In the law of the prophets,
Stoning must be done!"

Jesus, Son of Mary,
Wrote on the ground;
Not looking at the Pharisees,
Not making a sound!

The Pharisees kept asking,
Trying to trick,
But Jesus looked up calmly,
His answer was slick!

"He that is without sin among you,
Let him first cast a stone!"
Pricked by their consciences,
They made their way home!

He looked at the woman,
"Where are those who accuse?
Has no man condemned you?"
She said, with nothing to lose -

"No man, My Lord,
Accused me, I am sure!"
"Neither do I condemn you!
Go and sin no more!"

THE SAMARITAN WOMAN

All alone by the well, He sat
With nothing to draw the water,
But soon there came a woman there:
A shameful Samaritan daughter.

"Give Me a drink, for I have no jar –
I cannot reach the water!"
"Why do You speak to me?" she gasped,
"For I am a Samaritan daughter!"

"If you knew the gift of God
I could give you living water.
No longer would you thirst again,
You precious, Samaritan daughter!"

"Please, kind Sir, I'd love this gift,
So I wouldn't need to draw this water.
I would love the gift of eternal life.
Although I'm a Samaritan daughter!"

"Go and fetch your husband here!"
"But I have not one!"
"Five you've had – your words are true!"
Said God's eternal Son!

He knew her heart; He knew her life
Had been one of utter shame!
But ALL are saved who come to Him,
And call upon His name!

She knew this Man who spoke to her
Was different from the rest!
Her life she gave to the Lord
To be full of joy, and blessed!

We come to Him, just as we are –
Nothing can ever be done,
Because the work at Calvary
Was finished by God's own Son!

THE DYING DAUGHTER

She lay there on her sick bed,
Sweat drops on her brow!
Her father was in anguish –
She must be healed right now!

Her skin was pale; her body weak;
She found it hard to breathe!
Jairus had tried everything,
But nothing brought relief!

He sat there on his daughter's bed –
A tear fell from his eye!
He watched her life slowly slip away.
He prayed to God, "Oh why?"

He ruled the local synagogue;
He prayed three times a day!
Why did God want to take
His little girl away?

He'd heard about a Teacher –
One they said could heal!
But could he risk going to Him;
How would the Pharisees feel?

They would not want him to go
To the One they call the Christ!
But Jairus loved his daughter so;
He wanted to give her life!

Then he heard a terrific noise;
The news was spreading around!
Jesus, the Great Physician,
Was coming to his town!

His only hope was to find this Man
Who could fully heal his child!
He had heard so much about Him;
How He was gentle, loving and mild!

Pushing through the excited crowds,
He found Jesus and fell at His feet!
He begged and pleaded for Jesus to come
And make his daughter complete!

Jesus set off to the house
But people thronged around!
Pushing; shoving from everywhere –
No quick way could be found!

Jairus wanted to get home quickly!
His daughter lay near death,
For every minute that went by
Could be her final breath!

Suddenly the Teacher stopped!
Why does He linger so?
"Who has touched Me?" were His words,
"Who has touched My robe?"

Jairus wondered why He'd stopped;
Time wasn't on his side!
His daughter lay there weak and ill –
Perhaps she'd already died!

The woman knelt at Jesus' feet.
"Sir, I touched Your hem,
Then suddenly I felt Your power –
I'm fully healed again!"

"My dear daughter, don't you tremble –
New life begins right here!
Your faith has healed you of this ill –
Go, and do not fear!"

Suddenly, while Jesus spoke,
A servant came and cried,
"You need not bother the Teacher now,
For your beloved daughter's died!"

The mourners wept; the mourners wailed!
They told Jesus He was too late!
The little girl had passed away –
That was her awful fate!

But Jesus turned to them and said,
"She is not dead, but sleeping!
Why have you come to this place
With your wailing and your weeping?"

Jesus took Jairus' arm,
"Do not fear, only believe;
Your daughter is not dead, you see,
Because I can make her live!"

In the house the Master saw
The mother, tears in her eyes!
Jesus took the girl's hand
And said, "Dear child, arise!"

She opened her eyes and sat up.
Her Healer she could see.
Jesus turned to Jairus,
"A secret this must be!

"Now fetch your child some food to eat
And give her some refreshing water!
Go, praise God for all He's done;
For giving you back your daughter!"

Jesus is the only One
With power over life and death!
He came, you see, to Calvary
To give us spiritual breath!

WHO IS THIS MAN CALLED JESUS?

Who is this Man called Jesus?
Why did He have to die?
It seems a waste
Of a good Man's life!
I want to ask you – why?

Who is this Man called Jesus?
What is His life to me?
He was a good Teacher
And Healer,
Who died at Calvary!

Who is this Man called Jesus?
He lived so long ago!
How can He
Change my life?
I really want to know!

Who is this Man called Jesus?
What made Him best of all?
How can I
Hear Him?
Will He ever call?

Who is this Man called Jesus?
Why did He come to earth?
What do you mean
I can be born again;
I can have a new birth?

I do not understand this Man
Who came to deal with sin!
You mean I can be forgiven
If I will ask Him in?

Why would He want to save me?
Everything I lack!
My inward thoughts are
not the best
And my heart is black as black!

You mean He really loves me
Despite what I have done?
He has set His love
Upon me?
God's eternal Son?

You cannot work to get to Him!
Just going to church won't do!
He wants a personal relationship
With just Him and you!

So lay aside the things you love –
Throw them all away,
For the One who died
to save you
Loves you this very day!

A NOTE ON THE FOLLOWING POEMS:

These aren't Christian poems, but ones about life.

I felt 'inspired' (if that's the correct word) to write some of them, after the passing of some famous people who were quite young!

I've decided to include them in here because life isn't always plain sailing – it is often filled with much sorrow, many trials and temptations. Of course, it is also filled with much joy too (I have a couple of poems where I remember the fun of childhood)

As a Christian, I can recommend coming to Christ if you haven't already, because He is the only One who can heal our hurts (not necessarily instantly, but by leaning on Him and trusting in Him, it definitely helps us through our struggles). He, and He alone, can change hearts and make us new creations.

None of the poems have been endorsed by the companies mentioned!

MAKIN' TRACKS

Lookin' in the mirror, wanna look like my mummy;
Lipstick on my face, lookin' very funny -
When I grow up, wanna make lots of money!
Wanna be a superstar,
Wanna be a pop star!

High hopes, makin' tracks -
Wanna be famous;
Don' wanna go back
To bein' nothin',
Nothin' at all.
I want loads of fans
And be standin' tall
Everythin' revolvin' 'round ME!

Lookin' in the mirror, fixin' my hair;
Goin' on the stage, all my friends are there!
Livin' my life as if I don' care
Gonna be a superstar,
Gonna be a pop star!

In a studio makin' tracks -
Gonna be famous;
Don' wanna go back
To bein' nothin'
Nothin' at all.
I want loads of fans
And be standin' tall -
Everythin' revolvin' round ME!

Lookin' in the camera, paps in my face.
Night on the town; I act a disgrace!
Smokin' the dragon; I like to chase!
Wish I was no superstar,
Wish I was no pop star!

Somebody stop me in my tracks!
Do I wanna be famous?
Please let me go back
To bein' nothin'
Nothin' at all,
Where nobody knew me;
Where I could be small!

Lookin' in the mirror, high as a kite -
Snortin' coke, injectin' China White!
I begin to feel like Dynamite!
Never thought I'd go this far;
Do I wanna be a star?

Makin' tracks with a heroin needle,
Doin' drugs - an unnecessary evil
It ain't good 'cos it's illegal!
I really wanna go back
To bein' nothin'
Nothin' at all,
Where nobody knew me;
Where I could be small!

Lookin' in my coffin, tears in their eyes,
Deep in their heart it was no surprise -
They really wished I had been wise!
They never thought I'd go this far!
They always thought I'd be a star!

*Wheels under my casket, making tracks
To the six foot hole, deep and black!
They all wanted me to go back
To bein' nothin'
Nothin' at all,
Where nobody knew me;
Where I could be small!*

FAME AND FORTUNE

You took me to a mountain top
To show me earth's span.
You said I'd be adored
By every woman; every man.
You said I could party
Until the night was through,
So long as I gave up my soul
And only worshipped you!

You said I could have riches;
A manager and new friends;
Massive houses; loads of diamonds;
Lots of Mercedes-Benz.
You said I could have anything
This world could offer me;
I could be my own person;
Independent, cool and free.

So I gave up all my old friends;
Got new ones - just like me;
Rich, with massive houses;
Footloose and fancy free.
I thought I had the world's attention;
I began to worship fame!
My attitude was changing -
I got a brand new name.

I partied through the darkness;
I thought that I felt whole,
But the dark was not outside me;
It filled up all my soul.
I thought I had my life together;
I was on a fairground ride -
But it was so far from the truth;
I was dying from inside.

I spent all of my money
On cars and lots of jewels.
I declared myself bankrupt
Because I played the fool.
My new friends, they disowned me
Because my cash was spent;
Nothing now belonged to me -
I couldn't afford my rent.

The only friends I have now
Are my needle and my bong.
You told me I would rule the world,
But everything's gone wrong.
I've lost all my old friends;
My new ones have gone too,
Because I was so greedy
And I'd listened to you.

FOR THE LOVE OF MONEY

For the love of money is the root of all evil!
You'll do anything to get it, even if it's illegal!
Selling drugs to the young kids at the local school gate!
Your heart loves no people 'cos it's burning full of hate!

So long as you've got money, all you care about is **you**!
Behind you is destruction; murder; broken homes too!
Pros snorting coke - they sell themselves
to stay alive -
They have no other place to go; they please you to survive!

You think you're one hard man with your cash and your guns,
Your women on the streets and your daily drug runs.
Surrounded by your bodyguards, doing what you say!
You're like a wild animal hunting for its prey.

It doesn't matter who you cross; one day ya gonna die,
Then you will see that your life was one immoral lie!
No more money; no more coke; no more women in your bed,
Cos there will be nothin' when ya stone cold dead!

SHALLOW LIFE

Your life is as shallow as a half dug grave;
With your smoking and your drinking and your drug-filled raves!
You think you're cool with your body full of rings;
With your implanted horns and the trash that you sing!

Your life's in the gutter - as base as can be;
With your swearing and your sex-talk and your blas-phem-y!
You think you're cool with your breasts hanging out;
With your mouth so vile as you scream and shout!

Your life is like rubbish that rots on a tip;
With your drinking binges, and your big fat spliff!
You think you're cool when you're high as a kite;
When you go down the town and you start some fights!

Your life will end in a lonely, black grave,
'Cos of your smoking and your drinking and your drug filled raves!
Nothing left behind but your bones and your rings;
Implanted horns, but no songs to sing!

Deeper than the gutter - your coffin will be!
No more swearing, no more sex-talk, no more blas-phem-y
No more low cut clothes with your breasts hanging out.
Silence, just silence; you won't scream or shout!

Your body will rot like rubbish on a tip;
Your time is done, like your burnt out spliff.
No more highs; no flying like a kite,
No more town trips and no more fights.

MISSING THE BEAT

Your mother throws you on the street
As soon as the sun will rise!
Bottle in her hand;
Glaze across her eyes.

There's one thing you've never known -
The beat of a loving heart;
To sing in tune with society -
Building walls becomes your art!

You look to all your friends
'Cos that's where you think you will find peace;
But will they really stick by you
When ya hunted by the police?

There's one thing you've never known…

You do not respect adults
'Cos of the void in your soul;
'Cos of the way your parents treat you;
They make you feel so low!

There's one thing you've never known…

You build up walls of resistance
'Cos your heart can't take the strain!
You've been hurt once too often;
Been left out in the rain.

There's one thing you've never known …

You do bad things to get noticed,
So the focus is on YOU!
But deep inside your heart
You haven't got a clue.

There's one thing you've never known …

There's One who can lift you from the pit
Of anger and despair!
One who loves with ALL His heart,
And for YOU is always there!

*There's one thing you've never known -
The beat of His loving heart;
To be able to sing in tune to Him;
You can be set apart.*

LOST LOVE, LOST LIFE

As I sat on the platform
Waiting for my train,
Puddles like huge lakes
Made by lashing rain.
I looked up and I saw you,
Coat ragged and torn.
Whisky bottle in your hand -
Started drinking in the morn.

Lost love, lost life.
Losing all your money;
Losing kids and your wife.
Finding comfort in the bottle
And the voices in your head;
Begging on the platform,
Although your spirit's dead.

Eyes are so empty,
Hiding so much pain.
Wishing you could go back
And start your life again.
Heart filled with bitterness;
So much pain in your soul;
No money to your name;
You cannot claim the dole.

Lost love, lost life…

People will not go near you;
They think you are a stain
On their cosy, comfortable lives -
To them you are a bane.
They do not know your past:
You had a job and a wife,
A big house in the country
And a very rich life.

Lost love, lost life...

You may not be the man I knew;
Your heart is filled with pain.
You may feel lost and empty
As you sit there in the rain.
But love is something you can find;
It isn't totally lost.
The greatest love which can be found
Is at the foot of the cross.

Great life, great love.
Ruler of the nations
Came to earth from heaven above.
He lived a life of poverty;
Had no pillow for His head.
He sat with social outcasts;
By compassion He was led.

LOOKING BACK

I looked in the mirror and what did I see?
But a lady with grey streaks, staring at me.
She had crow's feet in the corners of her eyes,
And big shopping bags, which was a surprise!

It only seemed like a year and a day
Since my pals called around and asked me to play;
With their long skipping ropes, and hula hoop rings,
Magnadoodles, gyroscopes and those funny springs

I remember the discos with bright spinning lights,
The hall full of teens, and the playground fights;
Marbles and 2 ball and, if we were lucky,
We'd go to the shop and buy some Slush Puppie©!

We'd go to the park and play on the train,
And climb the tall slide, over and over again.
We'd play in the street until it got darker;
We'd knock on the doors, we'd turn and we'd scarper!

We thought we were cool in our bell-bottomed trews,
Our wide collared blouses and our platform shoes.
We listened to groups who wrote their own songs;
We'd never heard of computers and we never wore thongs!

Gone are the days of a simple childhood,
When T.V. wasn't colour - well, we thought it good!
Now we have mobiles, computers and Wiis*(TM)*
Our lives seem so rushed; we don't take our ease!

So as I stared back, I gave a big grin,
As I just remembered the times I'd lived in!
The lady grinned back, and so I could see:
That lady with grey streaks really was me!

REMEMBER, REMEMBER

I remember, remember the fifth of November:
The kids on the corners with guys!
They'd ask for a penny,
And if they got any
Their faces would look so surprised!

I remember, remember the fifth of November:
The sparklers we'd all whizz around!
We'd write in the air,
Avoiding our hair,
Then toss them, burnt out, on the ground

I remember, remember the fifth of November:
The rockets would fly way up high!
The bonfire was huge;
Heat making us rouge!
With excitement you'd hear us all cry

I remember, remember the fifth of November:
The colours as bright as the sun.
Fireworks popped and whizzed
And sparkled and fizzed!
Oh, those nights were such fun!

INDEX OF POEMS

A Place Prepared	56
Arise	77
Based on Ezekiel 34	21
Based on Psalm 1:1-4	20
Based on Psalm 23	18
Based on Psalm 40	19
Be Not Ashamed	39
Be Strong and of Good Courage	40
Broken - Whole	85
Captivate	4
Caught	92
Christmas Time	60
Come Meet	52
Come See	6
Come to the Lord	42
Empty - Full	53
Fame and Fortune	106
Finding What You Will - And Won't	62
For the Love of Money	108
For What Does it Profit…	46
Gentle Baby - Dying Lamb - Risen Saviour	65
He Took on Flesh	54
Help Me to be More Christ-Like	43
I AM	8
I Come to the Cross	12
I Shall Want for Nothing	10
I Stood at the Foot of the Cruel Cross	11
I Will Rest in You Alone	78
Imagine	37
In Death - In Christ	44

Jesus, Rock of our Salvation	14
Looking at the Cross	76
Looking Back	114
Lost Love, Lost Life	112
Make Me…	15
Makin' Tracks	103
Master	83
Missing the Beat	110
Nothing but Christ is Worthy	5
O Little Star	57
Precious Sons of Gold	16
Remember, Remember	115
Ride On	23
Shallow Life	109
The Bride	24
The Bright Morning Star	64
The Chief Priest	47
The Dying Daughter	96
The Gift	48
The Gulf	29
The Journey	82
The New Covenant	31
The Night Before Christmas (1)	68
The Night Before Christmas (2)	71
The One	90
The Path We Tread	91
The Power of a Word	84
The Precious Gift	66
The Prince of Peace	73
The Samaritan Woman	94
The Saviour - My Hope	32
The Shepherds on the Hill	58

The True Wonder of Christmas	50
The Virtuous Woman	26
There is a Time	67
There is Forgiveness	33
There's No Room - There's Always Room	74
Upon the Cross	36
Who is This Man Called Jesus?	100
Would You Go Through This For Me?	79